FAILING
AT AGILE TRANSFORMATION

FAILING AT AGILE TRANSFORMATION

How to Sabotage Your Agile Journey

Kelly Brogdon Geyer

Copyright © 2019 by Kelly Brogdon Geyer

All rights reserved. This book or any portion thereof may not be reproduced or used in any manner whatsoever without the express written permission of the publisher except for the use of brief quotations in a book review.

ISBN-13: 9781793308504

DEDICATION

To my remarkable husband, Markus and my two spirited boys, Gavin and Maximilian. This would not have been possible without your love and support. You are my life and my inspiration every day.

TABLE OF CONTENTS

Preface   *ix*

Introduction   *xii*

Chapter 1.   *What is Agile?*   *1*
- 1.1   Agile Manifesto   2
- 1.2   Twelve Agile Principles   3
- 1.3   Agile Methodologies   5
- 1.4   Agile Practices   6
- 1.5   The Nutshell   7

Chapter 2.   *Culture Shock*   *8*

Chapter 3.   *The End is in Sight*   *12*
- 3.1   Are We There Yet?   13
- 3.2   Don't Make Me Turn This Car Around   14
- 3.3   Destination Unknown   15

Chapter 4.   *Muddy Water*   *16*
- 4.1   Expectation 1: All Aboard!   16
- 4.2   Expectation 2: Save Money   21
- 4.3   Expectation 3: Save Time   22
- 4.4   Expectation 4: Improve Quality   24

Chapter 5.   *Monkey See, Monkey Do*   *27*

Chapter 6.   *One Size Fits All*   *30*

Chapter 7.   *Control Freak*   *32*
- 7.1   Traditional Management   32

| 7.2 | Agile Management | 33 |

Chapter 8. Keep the Same Goal   35

8.1	Traditional Goal: Make Money	36
8.2	Agile Objective: Satisfy the Customer	38
8.3	People or Profits First?	40

Chapter 9. Dive in Head First   43

9.1	To Swim or Not to Swim	45
9.2	Cold Water	47
9.3	Don't Pee in the Pool	48

Chapter 10. Put a Bow on It   49

Appendix 1. References   51

Appendix 2. Author Bio   53

PREFACE

Hardwired to crave the expected, humans want routines. We like predictability. We have a desire to know what is coming next. Even if you are a thrill seeker, there are far more areas of your life than you think where habits are present.

If you drive to work every day, you probably take the same route with a few exceptions for traffic. You probably eat your meals at about the same time each day. Heck, you might even eat the same food each day. You drink your coffee the same way each morning. If you exercise, you probably work out at close to the same time every day. You probably do your household chores on some kind of predictable schedule. The list goes on. Holding on to routines and relying on the predictable are what create a sense of security in our minds. Without it, we feel uneasy, on edge, and out of balance.

What does this have to do with Agile transformation? More than you might think. All too often, organizations underestimate the difficulty of making this shift. I hesitate to call this a shift because it is more than that. What happens is nothing short of reinventing an entire organization from the ground up. Often overlooked or underestimated, this reorganization is complex and challenging. The "head honchos" believe they can dictate that their company is "going Agile" and things will automatically fall into place. Sound familiar? Yep. I have trudged my way through this agonizing transformation more than once and I have seen the same blunders and mistakes that I will discuss in the coming pages.

Those head honchos enlist the help of consultants and advisors to tell them what they need to do to make the company become Agile. This is the wrong approach because the head honchos put these things in place and then believe they *are* Agile. However, there is a very distinct difference between *doing* Agile and *being* Agile. These same head honchos are often *doing* Agile things while at the same time, doing the very things that are destructive in an environment where people are trying to move toward true agility.

After witnessing and experiencing this firsthand, I decided to write this book. It is important to learn about the various tools and processes that are available to help in your Agile journey but it is just as important to learn what to avoid and what to stop doing. I cannot give you the magic plan to make your transformation successful and painless but I can tell you what will hold you back in this voyage.

I am not an accomplished or even an experienced author. If you are expecting to read a professionally written and edited book, you might be disappointed. I am just a Scrum Master who wants to share my experience in hopes of helping a person or an organization.

Many thanks to someone who I consider as a professional mentor, Tom Schulenburg. Tom was my manager when our employer in Connecticut decided to become Agile. I blossomed from an IT Project Manager to a Scrum Master with Tom's guidance and support. We studied together and he was instrumental in boosting my confidence to pass the required exams. Aside from helping me in my Agile journey, he is also the best manager I have ever had and one of the smartest people I know.

- Kelly Geyer

INTRODUCTION

If you are reading this book, it might be safe to assume that you work for an organization that is considering Agile or has just made the decision to change the way they work and try out this Agile stuff. Chances are you might have even read the many books and resources that explain the right steps to make this transformation easy. I hate to do this to you. I hate to burst your bubble but this will not be easy.

The number of practices you can test out to assist you in your Agile journey are limitless. Unfortunately, the number of counterproductive assaults people perform during the journey are just as limitless. There are countless books, websites and blogs that will describe dozens and even hundreds of different techniques that can help you become Agile.

With so many available resources, making this transformation successful must be easy. Right? Wrong! The sad fact is that an organization can employ every single tip and trick out there and still fail at Agile. How can this happen if they do everything they are "supposed" to do? It can happen because shifting in this way is much more than simply changing *how* you do things. Becoming a living, breathing Agile organization involves changing *why* you do things. There must be a complete metamorphosis of the company culture. Management structure must change. You cannot simply implement this mindset into your existing structure. Individual roles need to change and responsibilities need to adjust. Some positions become obsolete.

Therefore, my advice to you is to read as many books and resources as you can about Agile transformation. Educate yourself on all the things people have tried that worked. Familiarize yourself with the Agile terminology and nifty lingo. However, I also have a word of caution: Do *not* assume that doing these things will make your organization Agile. Employees can do all the right things but if they are also doing things that are harmful and detrimental to the Agile mindset, the transformation may fail before it has had a chance to thrive. Do not let that happen. Do yourself a favor and continue reading to learn about many of things that organizations and employees do that hurt the efforts to become Agile. Then do yourself a favor and share this book with others within your organization who are making these mistakes.

CHAPTER 1. WHAT IS AGILE?

I would be remiss to write a book about Agile without providing a brief description of what it actually means to be Agile. Oxford dictionary defines agility as being "able to move quickly and easily" (Oxford Dictionary 2015). I will spare you the lengthy history lesson on how Agile for software development was born. I will let you in on a little secret and tell you that Agile is nothing new. The beginning concepts and ideas began as early as the 1930s with Walter Shewhart's PDCA (Shewhart, 1939) which is an iterative four-step method (plan-do-check-act or plan-do-check-adjust). Dozens of other methods and ideas followed and in 2001, a group of seventeen computer folks got together to figure out a better way to develop software and help others. From their retreat at a ski resort in Utah, the Agile Manifesto was officially born.

If you were searching for a book to learn every dirty detail of Agile and really get into the meat of it, you will be disappointed with this book. There are plenty of resources available already that can tell you all the "right" things to help you during this change. The purpose of this text is to warn you of the pitfalls and slip-ups that can set you back.

Over the years, I have heard the term Agile Methodology many times. Agile is not a methodology. Agile is the umbrella term that encompasses several different methodologies including Kanban, Scrum, XP, etc.

Agile is a mindset described by four values and defined by twelve principles. Again, Agile is a mindset. It is a way of thinking.

Do not make it complicated by thinking it is anything more than a philosophy but do not underestimate the difficulty in changing the way people think.

1.1 Agile Manifesto

There are four basic values of Agile described in the manifesto. These values promote a software development process that focuses on quality by creating products that meet customers' needs and expectations. Below is the Manifesto for Agile Software Development (Beck, et al., 2001).

*****

We are uncovering better ways of developing software by doing it and helping others do it. Through this work we have come to value:

Individuals and interactions over processes and tools
Working software over comprehensive documentation
Customer collaboration over contract negotiation
Responding to change over following a plan

That is, while there is value in the items on the right, we value the items on the left more.

*****

Originally geared toward software development, these values in the original manifesto can still apply even if you do not work in IT. Simply change "working software over comprehensive documentation" to "valuable outcomes over comprehensive documentation." The rest stays the same.

1.2 Twelve Agile Principles

The Agile mindset is defined by twelve principles based on the values outlined in the manifesto. Each of the following principles are related in some way to at least one of the four values described in the previous section.

1. Our highest priority is to satisfy the customer through early and continuous delivery of valuable software.
2. Welcome changing requirements, even late in development. Agile processes harness change for the customer's competitive advantage.
3. Deliver working software frequently, from a couple of weeks to a couple of months, with a preference to the shorter timescale.
4. Business people and developers must work together daily throughout the project.
5. Build projects around motivated individuals. Give them the environment and support they need, and trust them to get the job done.
6. The most efficient and effective method of conveying information to and within a development team is face-to-face conversation.
7. Working software is the primary measure of progress.
8. Agile processes promote sustainable development. The sponsors, developers, and users should be able to maintain a constant pace indefinitely.
9. Continuous attention to technical excellence and good design enhances agility.

10. Simplicity--the art of maximizing the amount of work not done--is essential.
11. The best architectures, requirements, and designs emerge from self-organizing teams.
12. At regular intervals, the team reflects on how to become more effective, then tunes and adjusts its behavior accordingly.

Just as the manifesto can be changed slightly to be useful to people who work in areas other than IT, the principles can also be changed slightly to appeal to a wider audience. The twelve principles below are very similar to the original Agile principles but are a little bit more appropriate for other areas of an organization (Perkin & Abraham, 2019).

1. The primary orientation is towards customer need delivered through constant improvement of customer experience.
2. Strategies and tactics are highly adaptive and responsive, and change is welcomed.
3. Iterative, sprint working delivers customer value through continuous progress and momentum.
4. Effective cross-functional collaboration, supported through clear intent, is critical for success.
5. Build companies with motivated individuals. Empower teams to deliver through a flexible working environment characterized by trust and comfort with dissent.
6. Bureaucracy and politics are minimized, co-location and face-to-face communication are maximized wherever possible.
7. Working outputs are the optimum measure of progress and success.

8. Agile business supports relentless and sustainable innovation and progress. Change and iteration is constant, and the pace of progress never slows.
9. Technical excellence and good design are central to maintaining pace and agility.
10. Minimize wasted effort, duplication and resources.
11. The best results emerge from small teams with a high degree of autonomy.
12. Continuous improvement is achieved through embedded reflection time, and behaviors and culture that support learning.

For the seventh principle, I am going to be bold and say that "working outputs" should be changed to "valuable outcomes."

1.3 Agile Methodologies

Agile software development uses several different methodologies but there are a few defining traits of each one. Generally, one could consider any methodology that embodies the spirit of the manifesto and the twelve principles to be Agile. Some of the more important traits include:

- Short iteration cycles
- Focus on customer satisfaction through early involvement and continuous feedback
- Motivated and self-organized teams
- An effort towards daily face-to-face communication

The list of different methodologies is constantly growing. Some of the more familiar methodologies include:

- Extreme Programming (XP)
- Scrum
- Dynamic Software Development Method (DSDM)
- Adaptive Software Development (ASD)
- Crystal
- Feature-Driven Development
- Pragmatic Programming
- Lean Development

The type of methodology an organization chooses should depend on various factors including the type of product they sell, amount of investment the company is willing to invest, existing processes and procedures, criticality of projects, size of projects, how frequently requirements change, etc.

1.4 Agile Practices

Within the several different methodologies, there are numerous practices that teams use to become Agile. To handle requirements, teams may use a Product Backlog, User Stories and sizing, planning poker, refinements, etc. To tackle design, teams may practice spikes, emergent design, CRC cards, etc. As teams develop software, there are many practices used including coding guidelines and standards, Test Driven Development, pairing, refactoring, continuous integration, code reviews, metrics, version control, issue or bug tracking, frequent releases, etc. Teams manage testing with automation, acceptance criteria, unit testing, integration testing, etc. Time boxing, iteration planning, task boards, velocity, definition of done, burn down charts, and retrospectives are several practices for handling processes.

Organizationally, small teams should sit together, work at a sustainable pace, and may have a Scrum Master.

Agile teams may use any combination of these practices. They most certainly do not need to use all of them.

1.5 The Nutshell

This first chapter has described Agile. This is it. It is not complicated. There is no need to complicate it. Agile is a mindset described by four values and defined by twelve principles. If this is so easy, how do people screw it up? Before we dive into that, let us first set the stage. For the sake of simplicity and because repeatedly using the words 'company' and 'organization' gets boring, let's pretend we are referring to a fictitious company called Nimble Company. Nancy Newbury is the owner of Nimble and she has been considering adopting Agile for her company.

CHAPTER 2.   CULTURE SHOCK

An organization is a living, breathing organism. There is movement, change, and life. The company culture is the personality of the organization. It encompasses values and behaviors that "contribute to the unique social and psychological environment of an organization" (Organizational Culture, 2018). Cultures emerge through a combination of values, beliefs, principles, management style, nationality, language, and so on.

Some companies are more formal in their dress code or policies and other companies are more relaxed with casual clothing and more freedom. Some have a strong team-based culture where communication and interactions occur throughout all levels while others have a more traditional or formal management style. Some offices have employees segregated into individual rooms and other work environments use an open space layout.

Furthermore, it is important to determine if an organization has a strong or weak culture. Strong does not necessarily equate to good nor does weak equate to bad. A strong company culture is one where the employees can easily identify and explain the culture where they work regardless of whether they feel positive or negative about it. A weak culture is one where an employee would have a difficult time describing the culture if someone asked.

Why does company culture matter? It matters because humans operate companies and each person tends to prefer a particular way of working. If you are someone who prefers to work independently, you will most likely not enjoy being somewhere that emphasizes teamwork. If you do not like to wear a suit and tie every day, you will probably be happier working for an employer with a more informal dress code.

Outcomes will be less than stellar when an employee's mindset or personality does not fit in with the company culture. They will be less happy, less productive and it will be more difficult for them to form positive relationships with coworkers. Dysfunctional company culture can take many forms:

- Employees show a lack of respect.
- Infighting is prevalent in meetings along with playing the "blame game."
- Shirking responsibility destroys productivity.
- Tyrants who lack true leadership skills manage the staff using command, control, fear and force.
- Employees remain stagnant in their current positions and easily grow bored.
- The market is volatile causing employees to be in constant fear of losing their jobs.
- Criminal behavior is at play.

Cultural dysfunction is a symptom of a company disease. Repairing it is nothing less than a colossal feat. If it were a person with diabetes or cancer, you would not threaten or bully them to get better. You would take them to a doctor to find the root cause of their illness and seek appropriate treatment. Unfortunately, many companies are unsuccessful at mending their culture. Failure occurs usually due to foolish approaches like threats, intimidation and pounding your proverbial fist.

A simple answer does not exist for how to fix culture because too many influential factors are at play. Instead of diving into the background to discover real solutions, the decision-makers in a company often assume that becoming Agile will magically solve these problems.

Do <u>not</u> get caught in this trap. Agile does not solve problems. On the contrary, it will shine a spotlight on them. After issues have surfaced and been exposed, it is still the responsibility of employees to solve the problems. Unfortunately, people will instinctively want to blame the spotlight rather than objectively examining the causes of the problem areas and evaluating to address them. Pointing the finger at Agile is akin to being diagnosed with lung cancer after smoking for 25 years and then blaming the doctor who diagnosed you.

Nancy Newbury at Nimble Company from the end of Chapter 1 wants to become Agile and one of the reasons is because the company culture is in desperate need of help. Colleagues do not communicate well with each other. The actions and behaviors of the company leaders do not reflect the values listed on Nimble's website. Employees do not respect or trust their managers and the managers are oppressive. In essence, nobody is happy.

Nancy decides to move forward with the Agile transformation without addressing the current company culture at Nimble. She instructs the managers to organize developers into Scrum teams and assign roles. She contracts a few consultants to teach the employees about Agile and Scrum and estimates the transformation will be complete in about one year. She continues working in the same way she worked before the change.

There are several things wrong with this approach. Namely, having a timeframe for the transformation is a huge mistake but we will get into that in the next chapter. The major sin Nancy is committing is asking everyone in the company to change but failing to change anything about the way she behaves, thinks or works. Cultural change starts at the top and Nancy has failed to lead the way. Attempting to enforce a change in mindset within Nimble without the owner and managers reflecting that change is like driving a car and expecting it to veer right without turning the steering wheel. After her one-year benchmark, she is disappointed in the transformation so far and she blames Agile.

According to McKinsey & Company, about 70% of transformations or change programs fail to achieve their goals (Ewenstein, Smith, & Sologar, 2015). The majority of these failures are attributable to employee resistance and lack of management support. Adopting an Agile mindset requires employee engagement and a complete change in management strategy. Without a culture conducive to Agility, your transformation could fail.

CHAPTER 3. THE END IS IN SIGHT

Nancy wants to complete the Agile transformation in one year. There is a major flaw in this approach. Remember that Agile is a mindset and a mindset is created by experiences. Experiences are constant and infinite. In summary, your Agile journey is never done.

Consider your personal mindset. Do you still think the same way you did 5 years ago? 10 years ago? 20 years ago? My guess is that there are many thoughts and beliefs you had years ago that have changed due to maturity, life experiences, trial and error, world events, etc. As a young adult, I thought it did not really matter what I did for a living as long as I made a lot of money. I bent over backwards at my job to climb the corporate ladder. After some time, I was earning a decent paycheck and I was miserable. I liked the company I worked for but hated my job. I made a major change, which required a momentary step down in salary. I was earning less money but I loved my job. I realized that money did not have the importance I once assigned to it. It was far more important to follow my passions and figure out a way to make the money work. My mindset changed.

This change took years. Furthermore, it would not have happened any faster if someone tried to force this change. It came because of various experiences and trials. Upon realizing I needed to change, I could not have predicted how long my journey would have taken. Moreover, I still cannot predict it because it is still happening. I continue to find new ways to enjoy my profession without much concern for money.

This is one example of a change in mindset. You cannot assign an end date to a change in personal mindset so it is unreasonable to try to assign an end date to a transformation as complex as an organization adopting an Agile mindset.

Nancy is setting herself up for disappointment by expecting Nimble to be Agile in one year. She is trying to adopt a new mindset but thinking the same old way. She is treating this transformation like a Waterfall project with a completion date.

The twelfth Agile principle states that teams should regularly reflect on how to become more effective, then adjust accordingly. This means you are constantly inspecting and adapting to improve. Like a shark, you have to keep moving to avoid sinking to the bottom. This is the concept of continuous improvement, which is a major component of Agile. If your Agile journey is "done" then you have stopped improving and you are no longer Agile.

3.1 Are We There Yet?

If you have ever been on a road trip, you understand the agony of children repeatedly asking if you are almost to your destination.

This is how it feels when owners or managers in an organization set an end date for Agility. They grow frustrated with the pace of progress as their projected completion date approaches but there is still so much room for improvement. They hammer employees with questions, "Are we there yet? How much more time will this take? Why is this taking so long?" Meanwhile, the employees are just trying to keep driving without falling asleep at the wheel or succumbing to severe road rage.

To complicate things even further, managers will be frustrated that the company is not Agile "enough" yet but when asked what still needs to happen, they do not have an answer. They do not know where they want to go but they know they are not there yet.

3.2 Don't Make Me Turn This Car Around

The constant questioning about their timeframe discourages employees. As parents do sometimes, they threaten to turn the car around and go back home.

Colleagues reminisce about the good ol' days before Agile. They quickly and easily forget the pains of longwinded analysis sessions, lengthy design discussions, requirements gathering, inaccurate estimates, change requests late in the game, and testing large chunks of code for weeks at a time.

They do not like their managers breathing down their necks to transform faster. Huge shifts like this take time and everyone thought they were making good progress until their managers told them otherwise. Criticized for trying their best to adapt to this new way of thinking, they want to go back to the old way. Mutiny is near. They want to turn the car around and go back home.

3.3 Destination Unknown

Another downfall of treating this as a Waterfall project with an expected outcome and end date is that projects have a particular goal. However, Agile transformation is not a project.

Agile is a continuous journey. We are still on our road trip with the kids except there is a catch…we do not have a map or a GPS. Even more terrifying, we do not have a final destination.

We just need to continue driving around while trying to find the smoothest roads, most efficient car, least amount of traffic, and the cheapest car wash. Along the way, we stop to take pictures and discuss wrong turns, plan which direction we want to try next and fix the little irritating noise coming from under the hood of the car. At the same time, everyone in the car needs to get along and play well together.

CHAPTER 4. MUDDY WATER

Expectations are one of the worst nightmares during an Agile transformation. Business owners and managers will dive in with unclear and unrealistic expectations of what will happen in the coming weeks and months. Essentially, they "muddy the waters." There are numerous benefits to being Agile and there is an expectation that those benefits will surface quickly. Some positive results will appear quickly but most will take quite a bit of time or may not happen at all. That does not mean it was a bad decision to become Agile.

4.1   Expectation 1: All Aboard!

Assuming everyone in the organization will embrace boarding the Agile train is one of the most dangerous mistakes I've seen organizations make. They use the same methods they have used in the past to enforce change.

Last year, Nancy decided she wanted to reorganize a few of her departments at Nimble. She drafted a new organizational chart and disseminated it to the staff. Without any input from her employees, she made the decision alone. Everyone reorganized into his or her new departments because they had no choice. A few people griped to fellow employees but that was the extent of the issues.

Typically, this is the same approach used when organizations decide to adopt Agile. Often overlooked by management, obtaining employee buy-in is critical to being successful in this journey. Employees resist Agile transformations for a variety of reasons but according to a 2016 study published by Computers in Human Behavior (Gandomani & Nafchi, 2016), there are five key factors that contribute to resistance to change in organizations:

4.1.1 Lack of knowledge

Change will be unsuccessful if the employees are unclear of what they are doing and why. Organizations usually allow a few days of Agile training either online or in-person. This training usually touches on the basics of Agile, what it is, and might even cover some common practices like daily scrums, Kanban boards, retrospectives and so on. Most likely, the information only explains what these things are but avoids getting into the heart of Agile mindsets, values and principles.

When people do not understand what they are doing or why they are doing it, there is a chain reaction of miscommunication, misunderstandings, unrealistic expectations and frustration. It destroys employee morale. People typically do not enjoy working in a way they do not understand. The more time passes in this stage of discomfort, the more people will resist adopting an Agile mindset.

4.1.2 Cultural issues

If your organization has a long history of traditional project management or traditional management in general, this transition will not be easy because the organization most likely has several processes and policies in place that do not fit in with an Agile mindset. Managers most likely rely on more of a command and control style rather than collaboration and leadership. There might be a history of finger pointing or lack of communication. These problems will be highlighted during an Agile transformation and will further encourage resistance to change unless they are addressed.

When owners and managers tell their employees to become Agile, they are essentially changing the working culture and structure. However, expecting employees to undergo this transformation without simultaneously updating company culture leads to resistance.

Organizations need to reevaluate their culture and values to bring them in line with Agile values and principles.

4.1.3 General dislike of change

In the preface of this book, I touched on the fact that humans crave habit and routine. This is true because we enjoy living in our comfort zone. Some people prefer the status quo even if that means employees are not able to work in the best way possible. Their preference for habits, tradition, and predictability inhibit their ability or willingness to change.

In addition to people who simply prefer the status quo, there is another group of individuals who will resist an Agile transformation out of fear. They have climbed the corporate ladder to sit comfortably in a position where they are able to manage people. They use a command and control style because they are in a position of power. They tell their employees what to do, how to do it and in what timeframe. A successful transformation allows an organization to separate managers from leaders. The managers who are incapable or unwilling to lead rather than control will fight back against this new change. Some will consciously or subconsciously sabotage efforts by insisting on following old policies or implementing new policies that are at odds with Agile principles and values.

Another subset of the group who fears change are the people who are afraid of losing their job. This is particularly true of software testers because of the strong emphasis on robust automated testing in Agile. They are afraid that if they focus their efforts on automating more and more testing, they will work themselves out of a job.

Change can cause stress and when people feel stressed, they crawl back into their comfort zone. They will revert to doing things the same old way rather than growing into their new role.

4.1.4 The wrong mindset

We just reviewed the different groups of people who do not like change. Much of this resistance is a result of people trying to change their behavior before changing their mindset.

Employees are usually averse to change because of a lack of knowledge. It is uncomfortable to do something that is unfamiliar. There needs to be extensive upfront training as well as ongoing support to help employees understand the reasons behind this change.

Managers will resist this change due to the fear of losing power and control. This group can be particularly difficult because there is a lack of published information on manager's roles in an Agile environment. If someone is accustomed to managing a certain way for years, who is demonstrating this new way to manage employees? This leadership needs to start at the top with the owners, C-level executives and directors. They must lead by example by exhibiting the very behaviors they want their managers to exhibit.

4.1.5 Lack of effective collaboration

There are countless reasons why there may be a lack of effective collaboration. One of the reasons stems from poor communication. This is a systemic issue. A breakdown in communication is the number 1 reason for divorce in the United States and it accounts for 67.5% of divorce cases (Laws.com, 2016). Interaction with other people begins essentially the moment we are born but very few of us ever learn the necessary skills of communicating openly, cooperating, and successfully working in groups or teams.

To complicate matters further during an Agile transformation, organizations take individuals who have grown accustomed to working independently and force them into teams. The IT professionals might have worked for years and even decades in their field without collaborating with many people. It is possible they chose their career path because they do not enjoy working in a team. A certain degree of egocentrism comes into play.

Many people also have a tendency to blame other people for mistakes or problems rather than accepting accountability or putting forth the effort toward a solution. This makes collaboration far more difficult. Experienced Agile Coaches are essential to help everyone learn how to work together.

4.2 Expectation 2: Save Money

One of the reasons many companies choose to adopt Agility is because they believe it will save money and they expect this result to happen quickly. This is not always the case. It depends on many different factors.

Waterfall projects are typically more expensive than Agile projects but they are so dissimilar that a direct comparison is almost impossible. Waterfall projects require a lot of time and money spent upfront before any actual work begins. It is possible to spend weeks and even months doing analysis and gathering requirements for a project that may become obsolete before any development ever gets underway. Even more devastating is when a company spends months of time and millions of dollars to develop a product that their end customers do not want!

Ford Motor Company holds the prize for one of the most infamous product fails of all time. The company worked on the Edsel car model for about 2 years and produced 18 different versions (Deaton, 2018). Many factors led to this colossal failure. Quality and reliability issues wreaked havoc from the beginning. Priced higher than other Ford models at the time, the Edsel finally debuted when the United States was in the beginning stages of a recession. The price was not the only feature that was unattractive.

Aesthetically, consumers were not impressed with the large front grill. Critics claimed it resembled a toilet seat or even a vagina. The taillights were problematic because of their arrow shape, which pointed in the opposite direction. When the right turn signal flashed, the light appeared as an arrow pointing to the left. In total, Ford lost $250 million on the development, manufacturing and marketing for the Edsel.

The pure nature of Agile primarily eliminates these types of complications by working incrementally, delivering frequently, and receiving regular feedback from stakeholders and customers. If Ford was Agile, the Edsel story may have turned out very different. The vehicle may have still flopped but I would bet Ford would have lost far less money.

4.3 Expectation 3: Save Time

One of the dangers of expecting Agile projects to be completed faster than Waterfall projects is that it sets the development teams up for failure. Putting time pressures on Agile teams undermines the principles of Agile. Remember the eighth principle: "Agile processes promote sustainable development. The sponsors, developers, and users should be able to maintain a constant pace indefinitely." If teams are working 50-60 hours per week and racing against the clock to meet a deadline, this is not sustainable. There will be consequences.

Imagine Nancy at Nimble Company has a Waterfall project scheduled to last 6 months. Before the project begins, Nimble decides to use this project as their pilot Agile project. Nancy now expects the project to take only 4 or 5 months because she does not fully understand the Agile mindset yet. She is disappointed when the results of the projects are unsatisfactory due to ongoing bug fixes and conflicts within the development team. Nancy wonders how this could have happened.

Although she expects change throughout the organization, Nancy's own behavior has remained the same. She is continuing to push deadlines rather than focusing on quality and collaboration. The development team felt pressured to rush through their work and cut corners, which led to "code smell" and mistakes. They did not have enough time to collaborate with each other, which led to frustration and unclear acceptance criteria. The team is upset because they know a project like this should take a minimum of 6 months to complete properly. They do not feel empowered to determine the schedule.

The project meets their 5 month deadline but with poor quality and disengaged employees. The customer is unhappy. Nancy blames Agile!

What Nancy failed to understand is that even with the Waterfall timeline, this project did not dedicate enough time to development. Even if they used the Waterfall methodology, the project would have either been behind schedule or still had the same quality issues.

People often misunderstand the concept of early and continuous delivery. They mistakenly believe this means development will be faster. Logically, this does not make sense. If Feature A takes a developer one week to complete, that one week is the same regardless of whether you use Waterfall or Agile. To clear up any ambiguity, imagine Feature B should take 6 weeks to complete because it is more complicated and contains multiple components. Using Waterfall, the customer would wait 6 weeks to see anything. With Agile, the customer is involved daily with the team, has a chance to answer questions as the team is working on the feature, review the progress as components are ready and provide feedback. Feature B still takes 6 weeks to complete. Being Agile does not suddenly turn developers into super robots who can develop at lightning speed.

When someone puts pressure on teams to get work done faster, it has a negative impact on the team structure, self-organization, motivation and transparency. It also means there is a misunderstanding about what Agile does and what it does not do. The focus of Agile is not to be faster. The value in being Agile is better quality, higher value, frequent delivery and quick feedback.

4.4 Expectation 4: Improve Quality

One of the reasons Nancy wants to be Agile is because she wants to improve the quality of Nimble's products. She thinks that as soon as the teams are working iteratively and receiving regular feedback from customers, quality will improve.

The teams begin working in sprints and meeting with stakeholders and customers regularly to hear their thoughts. They quickly realize they need to focus more time and energy on automated testing, refactoring old code, continuous integration and extensive regression testing. They explain this to Nancy and tell her they will need to attend some classes to learn these new skills. They ask if she is willing to pay for the classes and if they are able to use a total of 3 days for learning. Nancy denies their request because she does not want to spend the money or lose 3 days of productivity. Unfortunately, quality does not improve, Nancy becomes irritated and the team grows frustrated.

This situation is all too real. Owners and managers tell their teams to focus on quality but then they refuse to provide the teams with the necessary time and tools to accomplish it.

The way in which you define quality needs to change. In traditional project management, quality means the product meets the specified requirements. On the other hand, being Agile means quality is defined a bit differently. Delivering a quality product means satisfying the customer with a valuable product. It is a subtle difference but an important one.

If this concept is still not clear, think back to the Ford Edsel flop. Ford built a quality product according to traditional methods. There were specifications for how the car should look, feel, perform and sound. Unfortunately, the Edsel failed despite satisfying all the requirements. From an Agile standpoint, Ford did not produce a quality automobile because they delivered a product that did not provide value to customers.

There are a variety of Agile tools and processes that contribute to delivering a quality product. Early and continuous delivery is one tool. You see the impact of small changes immediately. Receiving frequent feedback enables teams to adapt quickly. Automated unit testing, well-defined acceptance criteria, test-driven development and sprint reviews are some of the tools that teams can use to improve quality.

Unfortunately, team members might need to learn these news skills. This can take time and money. Nancy needs to understand this if she wants quality to improve at Nimble.

CHAPTER 5.   MONKEY SEE, MONKEY DO

The saying "monkey see, monkey do" refers to learning by mimicry without understanding why it works or considering the consequences. Unfortunately, many organizations misguidedly behave this way when observing wildly successful companies like Facebook, Google, Spotify, Apple and Amazon. They study the various practices and systems in use and try to copy them in hopes of similar success. This does not work in other areas of life so I never understand why companies think it would work when it comes to Agile.

I experienced a hilariously tragic example of this on my younger son's third birthday. I threw a tractor party for him complete with wonderful John Deere vehicles and décor. I surfed the internet for weeks looking at these beautiful tractor cakes. I do not really love baking but we live in a small village so buying a custom cake is not so easy. I decided to step up to the challenge and make the cake myself trying to copy one cake in particular I found on Pinterest.   This thing turned out like one of those hilarious memes you see on Facebook. I forgot that grass-colored frosting was impossible to find in our little village so I had to make my own. It turned out bright neon green. I was not able to find Oreos to crush up to make the "dirt" so I had to use these substitute cookies that did not crush as well so instead of dirt, it looked like giant brown rocks. I bought the tractor cake topper online and the metric system must have confused me because it was not the appropriate size for a sheet cake.

I learned some lessons. The cake tasted fine but it looked like a disaster because I did not consider the availability of the ingredients where I live and I also ignored my own lack of artistic abilities. Obviously, the person who made the original Pinterest cake I tried to copy was experienced at decorating cakes and had access to the necessary ingredients.

Just like people, every organization is unique and special. There are too many variables to copy an idea and expect the same result. The culture may be different. The people who work there probably have different skills, abilities and personalities. Customers most certainly have different wants and needs.

Do not interpret this message incorrectly. Do not ignore what other companies are doing. On the contrary, learn as much as you can about the various ideas from different companies in different industries. However, in order for that information to be useful, there needs to be an understanding of *why* it worked for them.

Before implementing new ideas and practices, organizations must ask themselves these questions:

1. Does this align with our company culture or the culture we are trying to achieve?
2. Does this solution fit into our environment?
3. Is this proposal appropriate for our products or services?
4. Will our leaders embrace this change and be ambassadors?
5. Can we provide ongoing support to continue in this direction?

If the answer to any of these questions is 'no,' serious thought should be given before proceeding. Know the core strengths of your company and capitalize on them. Do not attempt to implement a strategy just because it led to success somewhere else. Many factors determine success including market conditions, brand recognition, pricing, marketing, economic environment, and pure luck.

CHAPTER 6.   ONE SIZE FITS ALL

Using a one-size-fits-all approach is detrimental. Operating under the assumption that one strategy is suitable for all projects, teams or circumstances is a clear indication that there is still a lack of understanding about what it means to be Agile. It is a mindset, not a cure-all prescription.

During the beginning phases of a transformation, organizations enforce a host of Agile practices and tools. Most of the time, they force the IT department into Scrum Teams, make everyone use the same software like Jira, and ensure everyone holds their daily scrums and other events. There are so many tools to choose from, it is not necessary to force everyone to wear the same hat.

Depending on the deliverables and functions in different areas, some teams would work better as a Kanban team. Other teams would function better as a Scrum team. Still other teams may benefit from organizing as some combination of Scrum and Kanban or using a completely different methodology. Some teams may find dailies helpful but do not necessarily find value in structured sprint planning because of the nature of their work. Various teams use physical boards to visualize what needs to be done and other teams utilize technology.

Imposing these practices on employees leads to pushback. Forced to fit into a mold that does not make sense for their deliverables, they resist the adoption of Agile because they have no control over how they accomplish their work. They will revert to their old routines and processes.

One of the benefits for Agile teams is that they should be enabled to get the work done in the best way *they* decide. The teams need the freedom to decide the length of their iterations, how they track their work, which planning method they use, etc. However, traditional organizations are not accustomed to allowing this sort of independence. This change will require a shift in management style, which we will discuss in the next chapter.

CHAPTER 7. CONTROL FREAK

Traditional managers are used to telling their employees what to do and how to do it. Then they waste several hours per week checking numerous reports and metrics to babysit everyone rather than trusting employees to do their jobs.

Often overlooked, management style plays a huge role during a transformation. It is likely that the management culture in an organization will need a complete overhaul because Agile management is quite different from traditional management.

7.1 Traditional Management

Characterized by command and control, traditional management is certainly the most common management style in many organizations. My assumption is because it is the easiest to implement and monitor. It requires few skills and even fewer leadership qualities.

Currently, the managers at Nimble employ traditional strategies. Nancy tells them what to do and how she wants it done. They follow through by telling their employees what to do and how to do it. People fear losing their jobs so they do what their manager tells them to do. The management style at the company exhibits:

- Clearly defined job descriptions
- Delegated authority
- Hierarchical decision-making
- Bureaucracy
- Driven by processes and results

- Management motivated by power and career advancement
- Top-down command and control
- Goals and rewards focused on sales, profit, policy and output

Things are done the way Nancy wants so she assumes this style is good. Unfortunately, this style cannot survive in an Agile environment. There will be constant conflict between managers and employees. The only people who favor this style are controlling managers and owners who do not trust people. Employees dislike it because they are not able to do their best work.

7.2 Agile Management

Nancy reads a book about some things she can change to help the managers at Nimble use more Agile management strategies. Agile management will require Nimble to implement:

- Roles defined around work
- Authentic and transformational environment
- Flexibility and adaptability
- Collaboration and mindfulness
- Empowered employees and teams
- Objectives and rewards focused on team performance and enhancing skills

Having roles defined around the work instead of clearly defined job descriptions will allow the organization to adapt without the need to hire new people to acquire new skills. Having an authentic and transformational environment will breed trust and openness. Focusing on collaboration instead of top-down command and control leads to higher levels of employee engagement and alignment.

In my experience, empowering employees is one of the most difficult challenges for traditional managers. Put simply, they freak out. Remember, they tend to be the control freaks. They are still afraid of failure. They are afraid of losing their jobs because, so far, they have been the person making the decisions. They feel a lack of purpose. One way to overcome this is to let them know they still have a purpose. It is just a different purpose. Instead of a dictator, they are now more of a coach. They are there to support their employees. Do they need more training? Better software? A faster server? A more conducive work environment with bigger monitors or air conditioning? Of course, everyone has to work within budget and legal constraints. The key is to keep the lines of communication open.

Another major challenge faced by organizations is how to handle rewards or bonuses. In a traditional structure, employees get bonuses or a higher salary based on individual performance. This area needs to change once Agile teams are formed. It is unrealistic to expect individuals to work together effectively as a team if they still get rewarded based on individual successes. Convert the bonus or reward structure to a more team-based approach. Failure to make this shift will result in employees underperforming due to a lack of incentive.

CHAPTER 8. KEEP THE SAME GOAL

To further add to the complexity of all the facets of an organization that will be impacted by an Agile transformation, there also needs to be a shift in how work is planned. With Waterfall projects, there is an estimated cost and estimated schedule (time). Scope is supposedly fixed and there should be a focus on quality. Inevitably as the project progresses, stakeholders request changes, the work falls behind schedule, and costs differ from the estimate. One of the first aspects to suffer is

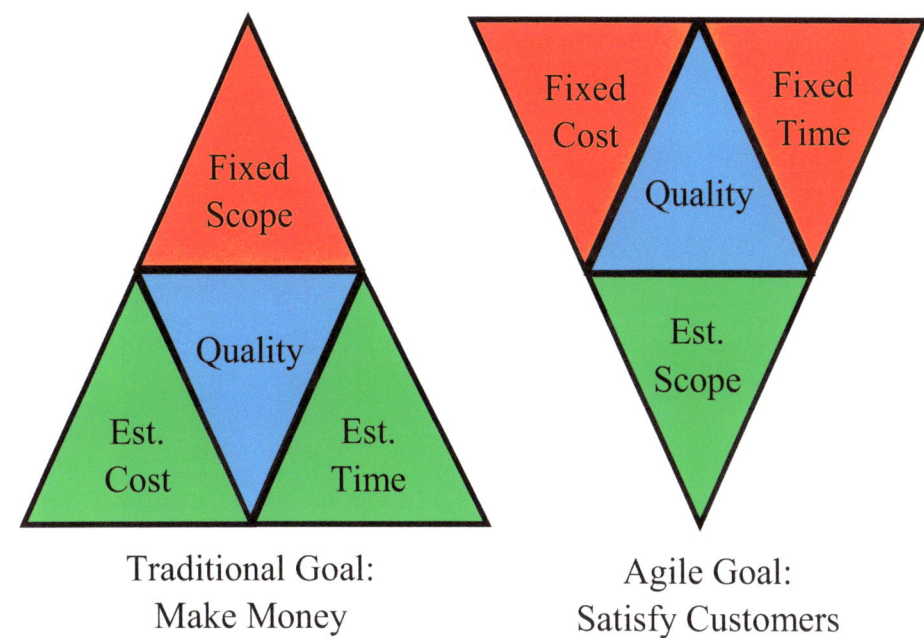

Traditional Goal:
Make Money

Agile Goal:
Satisfy Customers

quality. Reducing time for testing becomes a reality in order to meet deadlines for milestones. Using lower quality products for production becomes a possibility to cut costs.

In an Agile environment, things are a bit different. Costs are fixed because an Agile team with stable membership costs the same amount for every sprint. There is most likely a fixed launch date or even a mandatory date to meet regulatory or legal obligations. The heart and soul of Agile is the focus on satisfying customers with quality so lowering standards should not be an option. Quality is fixed. In this environment, scope is not fixed. It is flexible. When the launch date approaches, the team will release the quality product with the completed features. Some features (or part of the scope) may be incomplete so they will have to be included in future releases. You do not cut corners and sacrifice quality for the sake of including 100% of the scope.

This is a difficult adjustment for any organization. To boil it down in simple terms, the reason for the company's existence needs to change. Instead of existing with the goal of making money, the company must exist with the goal of satisfying customers. Read that sentence again. Companies that change the way they plan but do not change their goal are bound to face unnecessary challenges.

The next two sections of this chapter will describe the situations more clearly in terms of a project.

8.1 Traditional Goal: Make Money

Nimble Company has completed hundreds of "successful" Waterfall projects. Unfortunately, quality has always suffered. Nancy examines the last project they completed in an attempt to find the cause.

The Nim Widget project started with an estimated budget of $1.5 million and an estimated completion date of September 6th. The expected profits from this new product should surpass $3.6 million in the first six months. The fixed scope includes the finished product with ten features.

Unfortunately, during the course of the project, there were a number of setbacks. The original supplier of some of the materials raised their prices. The engineers also ran into a problem with integrating two different parts into the product, which caused a schedule delay. Nancy insisted on adhering to the original cost and schedule estimates because paying more for materials would increase the budget and delaying the launch of the product would delay making a profit on it. These are unacceptable outcomes because the goal is to make money and to make as much of it as possible as quickly as possible.

Nimble used an inferior material to save money and reduced time for testing and quality control. The project completed on time and within budget. Unfortunately, hundreds of the products were damaged during shipping so customers returned them. The mediocre materials were not as durable as the top quality materials originally in the plan. Other customers returned their Nim Widget because it did not operate as expected. Some did not work at all. Without testing and quality control, these issues went unnoticed. Customers also disliked the color of the product and the sound it made.

Negative online reviews spread rapidly and new sales quickly dropped. Nimble only earned a profit of $1.6 million in the first six months. They made some money from this product but far less than expected and they now have a bad reputation for producing low quality products.

8.2 Agile Objective: Satisfy the Customer

Imagine for a moment that we live in a fantasy world where we can analyze two identical projects using two different strategies. In this scenario, Nimble produced the Nim product with their Kanban team, Yes We Kan! The budget was easy. Yes We Kan has six members and each member earns $2,500 per sprint. Hence, the labor budget is $15,000 per sprint. The materials will cost $1,350,000. The team believes they can deliver all ten features in ten sprints. The total budget for the entire project remains the same $1.5 million that it was as a Waterfall project.

Miraculously, in our fantasy world where we make a fair comparison between two identical projects, the same two issues surfaced with the prices increasing for the materials and the engineers running into problems with integrating parts.

After the first sprint, the team delivered the first version of the product with the first feature to stakeholders and a customer focus group to get feedback. Nobody liked the color that so the team decided to fix it in the next sprint along with delivering the next feature. At the next review, they presented the next feature and the new color and received positive feedback. This continued for the next several sprints. They found out about the increase in the price of materials for a key product part. One of the team members found a comparable replacement at a lower price for a different part of the product. They will use this savings to offset the increased price of the first part.

In the seventh sprint, the stakeholders and customers said they did not like the loud noise from the product so the team spent the next sprint fixing it and working on the next feature. They ran into the integration issue in the eighth sprint. It was resolved but it took more time than expected.

By the end of the eighth sprint, the team knew they would not complete all ten features by the expected launch date. They refused to cut corners to sacrifice quality. Together with the stakeholders, they make a decision to stick with the original launch date but with only nine out of the original ten planned features. They can always add this tenth feature in a new version or as an upgrade.

The team has been testing aggressively and continuously checking for quality. By the end of the tenth sprint, they delivered and launched a fully functional, high quality product.

Positive customer reviews flooded the internet. Sales surpassed expectations in the first six months. The team implemented the tenth feature along with two additional features. Nimble launched the new Nim II product and received more rave reviews.

They key concept here is satisfying customers. Yes We Kan refused to sacrifice quality. Even though they delivered a product with only nine out of the ten originally planned features, the customers were happy to get those nine features and the future customers were happy to pay a slightly higher price for the updated version with all ten features a few weeks later.

8.3   People or Profits First?

Take a moment and reread the twelve Agile principles that are at the beginning of this book. Now read the first principle again. Did you notice anything special? Not one principle focuses on making money or increasing profits or improving shareholder value. The first principle states: "Our highest priority is to satisfy the customer through early and continuous delivery of valuable software." Read that sentence one more time with a particular focus on the first eight words. Customer satisfaction is the *highest priority*.

There are various ways to satisfy customers. Making your employees happy is one of the best places to start. Organizations ignore this area too often. Managers treat employees poorly but wonder why customer satisfaction is low.

"The way you treat your employees is the way they will treat your customers." – Richard Branson

High customer satisfaction levels are impossible with unhappy employees. Some of the top reasons for employee dissatisfaction include:

- Being or feeling underpaid
- Feeling unappreciated
- Limited career growth and advancement
- Poor management and lack of leadership
- Lack of interest or meaningful work
- Absence of work and life balance
- Conflicts with coworkers

- Not enough perks
- Unsafe or unhealthy work environment

Employees cannot deliver excellent customer service and quality products if they are unhappy in their job. Abraham Maslow had a theory about the needs of humans. Maslow's hierarchy of needs (Maslow, 1943) is a theory of psychological health centered on fulfilling innate human needs before becoming motivated to achieve needs at the higher levels of the pyramid.

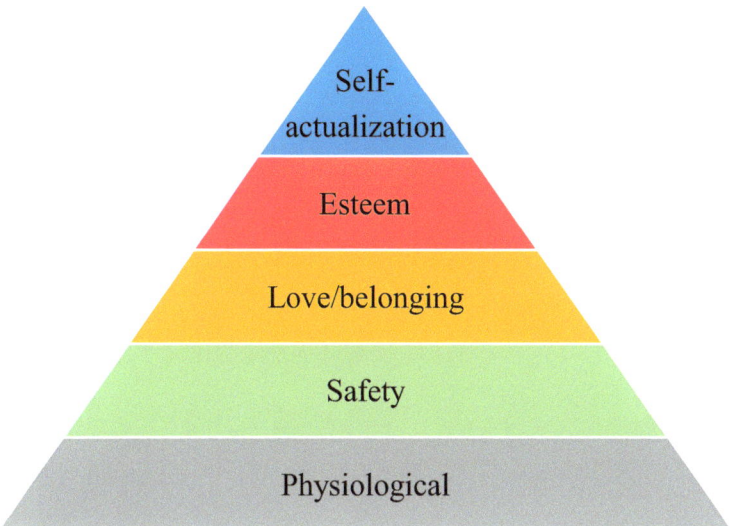

Physiological needs are basic requirements for survival such as food, water, sleep, and shelter. Once a person's physiological needs are satisfied, they will attempt to secure their safety. This need includes personal, emotional, financial and health security. After the fulfillment of physiological and safety needs, a person will seek feelings of love and belonging. He or she will cultivate friendships, intimacy and familial relationships. When a person has satisfied their physiological, safety and love needs, they will develop a desire for higher self-esteem and self-respect. People often engage in a profession or hobby to gain recognition, feel accepted or valued.

Behaviors at the top of the pyramid include using abilities and talents, pursuing goals and seeking happiness. These activities that help fulfill the need of self-actualization would help a person perform at a higher level as an employee. However, according to Maslow, a person will not focus on the need for self-actualization unless their other needs are met.

CHAPTER 9. DIVE IN HEAD FIRST

One thing I have seen organizations do is to jump head first into the Agile transformation. The Nimble Company was a victim of this strategy. Once Nancy finally made the decision to move forward with adopting this new mindset, she told the entire IT department to organize into Scrum teams and start "being Agile" immediately. While it's nice to be enthusiastic, I caution against this strategy. There is a reason for the "no diving" signs near some pools. There is too much danger and the risk for injury is too great.

One of the key ideas of being Agile involves making small, incremental changes and then inspecting the results. When you task an entire department of dozens or even hundreds of people with completely shifting the way they work, this is not a small change.

Nancy's decision to make everyone change at the same time caused chaos, frustration and resistance. There were no colleagues for people to turn to for help with the transformation. Nimble had a very difficult time finding enough Scrum Masters for all the teams. Training everyone at the same time was a monumental challenge and decreased productivity for the entire company. After a very short period of time, it was apparent that working in a Scrum team was not appropriate for some teams. Their work was not complex and did not change often. Everyone starts to question the decision to become Agile and they think it was a bad idea.

This is a common result when an organization employs the "all-in" approach. When you understand and embrace Agile, you understand this approach to becoming Agile is not ideal. Agility is about making those small changes, inspecting the results, reducing risk, adapting quickly, etc. There is another option in this journey.

Instead of diving into the Agile waters head first with no life preserver, try just dipping your toe in the water to test it out. Is the water too cold or too hot? Is it deep enough or too shallow? Is it polluted? Are there predators hidden beneath the surface?

The best chance of success lies in finding the people who are most likely to support this change. Find the employees who are enthusiastic about learning something new, comfortable taking risks and are social. These are your innovators. They are the people who wait in line for days at a time to be the first to buy the newest gadget or stand outside the movie theater to get the front row seat to the new cult classic. Teach them about the Agile mindset and give them the tools to work in this new way. Give them the support they need to be wildly successful. Encourage them to share their experiences, positive and negative, with other colleagues.

9.1 To Swim or Not to Swim

If we examine Everett Rogers' theory of the diffusion of innovations, we can see how and why new ideas can spread throughout an organization (Rogers, 1962). There will be people who are eager to try something different yet others who want to stick with the status quo. Some people are ready to jump into the water and others do not want to swim at all. A company will have better alignment and engagement with employees if the employees feel they have been part of the decision-making process to become Agile.

According to Rogers, there is a five-step process for making decisions and Nancy has decided to try to use this process to encourage her employees to become Agile.

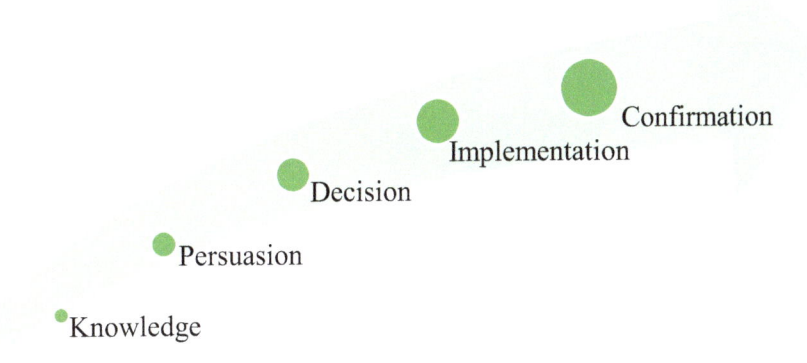

1. Knowledge (awareness): *a person is exposed to a new idea but does not have much information.* This is the stage where Nancy has discussed the idea of becoming Agile with the employees but nobody really knows much about it.

2. Persuasion (interest): *people become interested in the idea and actively seek information.* Many of the employees at Nimble approach Nancy and ask for some training and coaching about Agile, Scrum, Kanban, etc. Nancy hires coaches and pays for this group of employees to take some courses to learn more.

3. Decision (evaluation): *people will take the knowledge they have gained to make a decision whether to accept or reject the idea by weighing the advantages and disadvantages.* After learning more information, some of Nimble's employees decide they do not want to move forward with becoming Agile. This is okay. However, many employees have decided they want to make a change and they see many benefits to how they can improve by using some Agile tools and processes.

4. Implementation (trial): *carry out the idea.* Employees organize themselves into teams and start conducting small experiments like planning their work for the next two weeks, meeting daily for fifteen minutes to discuss if anything has changed, reflecting on the past two weeks to find areas to improve and so on.

5. Confirmation (adoption): *finalize the decision to continue with the new idea.* A few months after the initial trial period, several teams have found that this new way of working seems to be better for them. They decide to continue on their journey to becoming Agile.

9.2 Cold Water

Nimble has this passionate group of employees who are beginning to really enjoy working in an Agile way. Unfortunately, the waters are still a bit too cold for some of their colleagues and they are not as comfortable with their ability to swim. Nancy wants to warm up the water so she decides to try a few experiments of her own.

Nancy redesigns the office space. She takes down the cubicle walls and creates a more open atmosphere. She got rid of the large kitchen and installed several small kitchenettes with coffee stations throughout the office to encourage people to stop and chat with each other. Instead of only a few large conference rooms, she added dozens of small areas set up like living rooms with comfortable seating and natural light. Nancy talks with those early Agile adopters and encourages them to share as much as they can with their coworkers about their new journey.

The teams that initially began the transformation decided to hold an open space type of discussion and invited everyone at Nimble. They talked for about thirty minutes, sharing their experience and excitement and then allowed plenty of time for the attendees to ask questions. This discussion led to dozens of additional employees asking how they could get started making changes too.

Nancy was so happy with how things were coming along that she decided to take her entire group of Agile "cheerleaders" out to celebrate. They started the evening at a fun escape room where they collaborated together to solve puzzles and riddles. Then they went bowling and had dinner. On Monday morning, everyone gathered at the coffee stations to talk about how much fun they had.

Several colleagues overheard the conversations and were intrigued. They asked for help in learning more about Agile. They wanted to know which courses were most beneficial and which books people liked best. Nancy decided to form a small team of mentors from the original group who would offer to assist and coach newcomers along the way.

9.3 Don't Pee in the Pool

Eventually, the water temperatures rise and the majority of the company is swimming together in the Agile pool. Unfortunately, there are always people who resist change despite seeing and hearing about how successful the transformation has been for others. They will try to pollute the 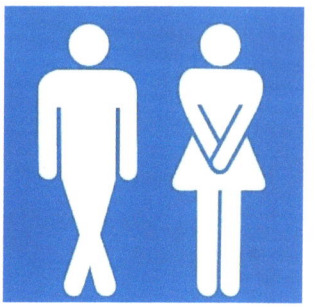 water but the other Nimble employees will not allow them to "pee in their pool" by spreading negativity.

When they overhear griping and complaining, they extend an invitation to sit and have a chat over coffee. They openly answer more personal and focused questions from the employees who have been fighting this change for so long. They calm more fears. They encourage trying to make small changes rather than big ones to ease the discomfort. The mentoring becomes an invaluable tool to get the last stragglers into the water.

CHAPTER 10.   PUT A BOW ON IT

I would love to wrap up this book, put a pretty bow on it and tell you that as long as you do not do the things I warned you about, your Agile journey is going to be a painless success. Unfortunately, it is not that easy. Changing the mindset of an entire organization, regardless of how big or small, is not a minor task. During your voyage, keep in mind:

- Agile will not fix a broken company culture.
- Do not treat this like a project with an end date.
- Eliminate unclear or unrealistic expectations.
- Your company may or may not realize a savings in time or money by deciding to become Agile.
- Quality improvement is not automatic.
- Do not assume everyone will enthusiastically want to join this excursion.
- Assuming you can copy the strategies that led to success for another company and expect success is silly.
- One size does not fit all.
- Get rid of command and control management. Let people know what you need done and then allow them the freedom and autonomy to do it the best way they can.
- An organization should exist to satisfy customers and this should lead to earning a profit, not the other way around.

- There is no need to make a huge organizational change in the beginning. Start small and allow the good word to spread organically.

This is not an exhaustive list. These are just things I have observed personally that hinder an organization's ability to make this transformation possible. It certainly does not mean that if these things are happening, the company is doomed for failure. These factors *could* sabotage the success of a potentially amazing transformation. At the very least, they do not help in moving it forward.

My hope is that this text helps shed some light on how to make things easier during a time that is sure to be uncomfortable for many people. As humans, we like comfort and predictability. We like to know we are doing a good job. We enjoy feeling knowledgeable. Avoiding risk is what has kept us from becoming extinct. I encourage company owners and managers to keep in mind that the work gets done by people who have emotions. Do not ignore this fact during your Agile transformation. Set yourself up for success by making this change fun. Make it collaborative, driven by quality, focused on people and make sure you do it incrementally.

Thank you so much for taking the time to learn about ways to save your organization from potential saboteurs. I hope that this information has been helpful, interesting and relevant. I wish you the best of luck on your own Agile journey.

APPENDIX 1. REFERENCES

Beck, K., Beedle, M., Bennekum, A. v., Cockburn, A., Cunningham, W., Fowler, M., . . . Thomas, D. (2001). Manifesto for Agile Software Development. Retrieved from http://www.agilemanifesto.org

Deaton, J. P. (2018, October 17). *Why the Ford Edsel Failed*. Retrieved from How Stuff Works: https://auto.howstuffworks.com/why-the-ford-edsel-failed.htm

Ewenstein, B., Smith, W., & Sologar, A. (2015, July). *Changing Change Management*. Retrieved from McKinsey & Company: https://www.mckinsey.com/featured-insights/leadership/changing-change-management

Gandomani, T. J., & Nafchi, M. Z. (2016, September). Agile transition and adoption human-related challenges and issues: A Grounded Theory approach. *Computers in Human Behavior, vol. 62*, 257-266.

Laws.com. (2016, October 25). *Divorce Laws*. Retrieved from Number One Reason for Divorce: https://divorce.laws.com/number-one-reason-for-divorce

Maslow, A. (1943). A theory of human motivation. *Psychological Review*, 370-396.

Organizational Culture. (2018, October 4). Retrieved from The Business Dictionary:

http://www.businessdictionary.com/definition/organizational-culture.html

Perkin, N., & Abraham, P. (2019, January). *The Agile Business Manifesto.* Retrieved from Building the Agile Business: http://agilebusinessmanifesto.com/agile-business-manifesto/

Rogers, E. M. (1962). *Diffusion of Innovations.* New York: Free Press of Glencoe.

Shewhart, W. A. (1939). *Statistical Method: From the Viewpoint of Quality Control.* Washington, DC: Graduate School, The Department of Agriculture.

APPENDIX 2. AUTHOR BIO

Kelly Lynn Brogdon Geyer has worked in project management since 2008 in financial services, construction, health insurance and telecommunications. She is a certified Project Management Professional (PMP®), Agile Certified Practitioner (ACP®), Certified Scrum Master (CSM®) and holds a Scaled Agile Framework (SAFe®) certification. Her focus is on guiding organizations and teams through the Agile transformation journey. She enjoys continuing to expand her own knowledge about the various tools, processes and resources available. Kelly grew up in southern California and then lived in central Connecticut for ten years before moving to lower Austria in 2017 where she lives with her husband and younger son.

www.ingramcontent.com/pod-product-compliance
Lightning Source LLC
Chambersburg PA
CBHW040234220526
45473CB00001B/232